STRUCTURE as design

ROCKPORT

STRUCTURE
AS DESIGN

GLOUCESTER MASSACHUSETTS

ROCKPORT
PUBLISHERS

23 Projects that Wed Structure and Interior Design

Isabel Allen

First published in the United States of America by
Rockport Publishers, Inc.
33 Commercial Street
Gloucester, Massachusetts 01930-5089
Telephone: (978) 282-9590
Facsimile: (978) 283-2742

ISBN 1-56496-604-6
10 9 8 7 6 5 4 3 2 1

Design: Stoltze Design
Cover photo: Timothy Hursley

Printed in China.

Contents

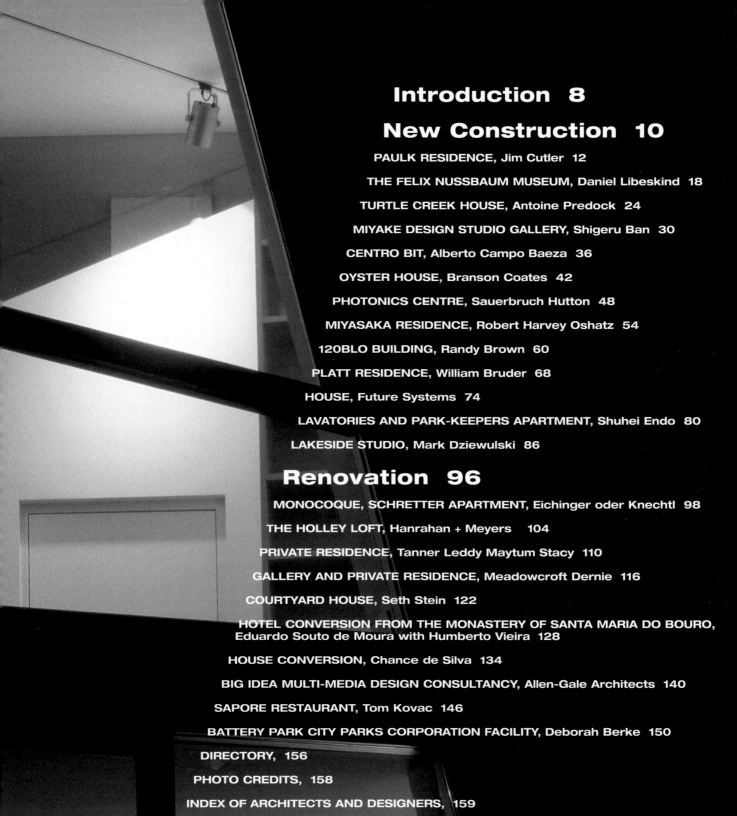

Introduction 8

New Construction 10

Renovation 96

Introduction

There are various methods of creating architectural design. Sometimes architects create a shell and decorate it to achieve the desired effect. Another method is to create a structural system whereby the structure is integral to the way the building looks. It is this second method that we will examine closely in the examples in this book.

Whether celebrating the tactile qualities of traditional building materials such as timber and stone, emphasizing the smooth precision of contemporary materials such as concrete, glass, and steel, or even experimenting with more unusual materials such as paper tubes or corrugated tin, all the architects featured in this book use structural elements as an integral part of the overall design. The first section looks at cases in which architects have produced an entirely new building: a dream home for a private client, office space for a commercial client, or even a building for public use. In designing private houses, a good working relationship with a sympathetic client has allowed these architects to create a series of highly customized interior spaces where every last detail has been thought of as a part of the overall vision. Those designing office spaces have risen to the challenge of producing a stimulating working environment where structure and services are a coherent part of the design, but are sufficiently flexible to allow for the needs of future users, while those designing public art galleries have produced spaces as lovingly crafted as the works of art they contain.

The second part of the book showcases examples for which architect were commissioned to work with existing buildings and looks at the extent to which the new interventions have been influenced by the structure and finishes of the existing space. Whether adapting an old building to a new use—a barn into a house, a monastery into a hotel—or simply transforming a space to suit the current user's needs and tastes, each of these designers has used an existing structure as a springboard to create a dramatic new environment.

While most of the projects featured in this book rely on the arrangement of walls and partitions, the choice of materials, and the use of transparency and light to generate a desired effect, otherprojects explore structural techniques that produce spaces that are themselves sculptural in shape. All the structures are characterized by the designer's ability to conceive of a building in its entirety. From the initial choice of materials to the treatment of lighting, heating, and ventilation, all have been designed as part of a coherent vision.

Whether the architect's intention was to create a space that is serene, slick, cozy, or dramatic, each has executed an environment where every last detail enhances the integrity of the design.

NEW CONSTRUCTION

In designing a new building, the choice of materials and the structural approach can have as much impact on the character of the interior as on the external appearance. Future Systems' London house and Mark Dziewulski's California studio both use modern materials—steel, concrete, aluminum, and glass—to create crisp, transparent structures. Others combine modern elements with more traditional materials: William Bruder's house in Arizona sets a delicate steel frame against massive walls of desert stone, while Antoine Predock's Dallas house contrasts lightweight planes with solid walls. Robert Harvey Oshatz's house in Japan and Jim Cutler's house in Washington both explore the structural possibilities of timber, creating homes that combine the familiar warmth of wood with eye-catching design. Whereas these houses respond to the site and to the client's tastes, Nigel Coates' prototypical Oyster House is not site-specific, and its interior can be altered to suit different needs.

Too often, public buildings end up as a compromise, but the architects featured in this book have managed to create workplaces that are also works of art. Alberto Campo Baeza's glass-walled office complex in Mallorca allows staff to enjoy views of a courtyard planted with orange trees, which are themselves aligned with the structural grid. Sauerbruch Hutton's Photonics Centre in Berlin meets complex practical requirements but is also a building of sculptural beauty, while Randy Brown's Omaha office building and Daniel Libeskind's Felix Nussbaum Museum in Germany are both composed of unpredictable interior spaces defined by sloping planes. Shuhei Endo uses corrugated tin to produce a park building that is spiral in shape, while Shigeru Ban's Tokyo gallery explores the structural qualities of cardboard tubes.

Jim Cutler
PAULK RESIDENCE
Seabeck, Washington

Jim Cutler's Paulk Residence looks as though it is part of
its natural surroundings, with timber elements used in a
way that echoes the random patterns of trees in the
surrounding forest. The structure is literally, as well as
metaphorically, respectful of the forest–only three trees
were felled, and at one point the roof and rafters were
notched to preserve a tree.

A 130-foot (39.6 m) -long wooden entry ramp supported by wood posts on concrete plinths leads to the glass-framed
entrance door, and passes through the house into the forest beyond, terminating in a belvedere perched high in the cliffs.
Although the house is anchored to the ground at its south end, the ground falls away at the north end, and the house is
supported by haphazardly arranged cross-braced posts. Exposed timber framing in the foyer is
asymmetrical, and floor joists are cut as random lengths. In places, the ceiling is pulled back to reveal the rafters. Maple
floors and pine paneling are treated with a transparent stain, and sheet metal is screwed into place as soffits or wall
panels. The rear elevation is a 22-foot (6.7 m) -tall grid of timber and glass that provides views of the water and trees.

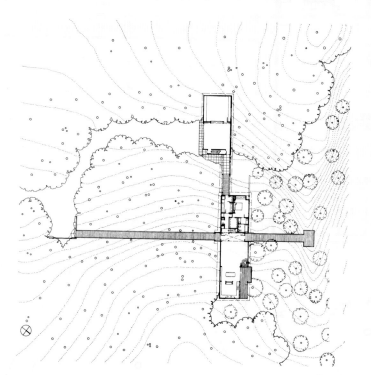

Exposed framing in the foyer echoes the random arrangement of the surrounding trees.

14

Floor joists are cut as random lengths.

Timber framing, maple floors, and pine paneling provide a warm internal finish.

The glass-framed front door is reached via a wooden ramp that floats over the contours of the site.

Upper-floor rooms are defined by the slope of the roof, which is oriented to take advantage of the views.

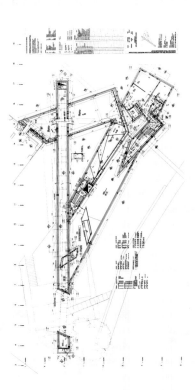

Daniel Libeskind
THE FELIX NUSSBAUM MUSEUM
Osnabruck, Germany

As a deconstructivist, Daniel Libeskind designs structures that challenge homogeneity and mediocrity. Built to display the works of Felix Nussbaum, a Jewish artist who died in the Auschwitz concentration camp in 1944, this building is deliberately disorienting. The visitor catches glimpses of rooms above or below through steel mesh panels set into the floors, but cannot necessarily see how to get to them. Sloping floors, angled walls, the seemingly arbitrary shapes and positions of windows, and lighting tracks that score the ceilings are based on a system of reference lines that symbolize Nussbaum's movement, displacement, and exile.

The triangular museum complex consists of three rectangular volumes, the largest of which has an oak-clad exterior cut open by asymmetrical windows and scored with oblique seams. The other two volumes include an elevated zinc-clad bridge linked to the existing Museum of Cultural History and a long, narrow, horizontal concrete monolith that encloses two corridors, one above the other, both dimly lit from above. A towerlike exhibition room is connected to the rest of the complex by a seventeenth-century arched bridge that was discovered during construction.

Controlled use of lighting lends the concrete corridor a sepulchral glow.

A metal walkway spans the restored vaults
of a seventeenth-century bridge, leading to
the entrance and to the concrete tower.

Wall planes are fractured by oblique window
slits, while ceilings are scored by lighting
tracks and–on the top floor–fissures of glass.

**Volumes are distorted by irregularly shaped
windows, raked floors, and angled walls.**

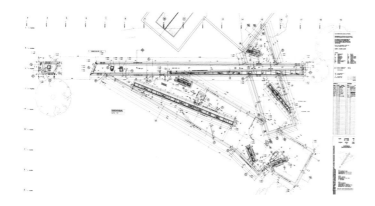

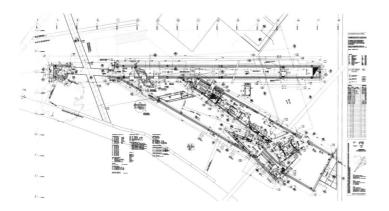

The vertical lines of the oak cladding are disrupted by asymmetrical windows and oblique seams.

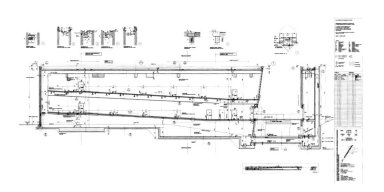

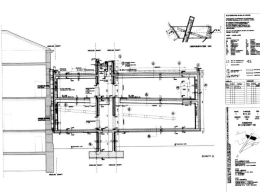

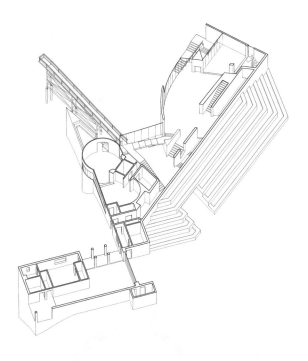

Antoine Predock
TURTLE CREEK HOUSE
Dallas, Texas

In designing Turtle Creek House, Antoine Predock created a solid front elevation that anchors the house to the landscape and a more open rear prospect that takes advantage of the view. Planted limestone terraces, which allude to the geological makeup of the ancient landscape, step up to the front elevation. From the street, the house reads as a solid mass of concrete and gray stucco, interrupted only by narrow strips of clerestory windows and deeply recessed glass doors. The entrance path burrows through the limestone to a central fissure, giving access to the two wings of the house and to the steel ramp that projects through trees and into the sky. Designed for enthusiastic bird-watchers, there is access to various observation points—a projecting sky ramp, rooftop walkways, and an intimate circular rooftop arena screened by a parapet wall.

The interior is composed of sharply angled, bright spaces, with huge glazed walls overlooking Turtle Creek. Different structural elements are separated from each other, so that walls hover above floors and metal staircases soar in front of glass walls. The surroundings are reflected in a mirrored steel plate on the rear elevation, so that a nearby tree becomes part of the facade.

The central fissure, formalized as an entrance foyer, is the point of access to the various observation points and to the north and south wings.

Solid planes are separated by gaps of 3 to 6 inches (7.6 to 15.2 cm), so that they appear to float in space.

The interior is composed of sharply angled,
bright spaces, with huge glass walls
overlooking Turtle Creek.

The openness of the largely glazed rear
elevation contrasts with the defensive solid
wall that overlooks the street.

Shigeru Ban
MIYAKE DESIGN STUDIO GALLERY
Tokyo, Japan

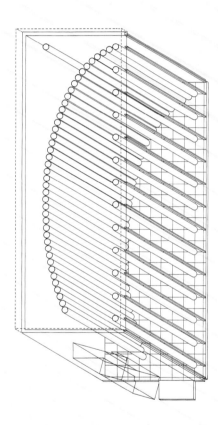

Shigeru Ban has designed a series of buildings in which he experiments with different materials. This gallery, built for exhibitions of work by young artists and designers, explores the structural possibilities of paper. The small rectangular pavilion has a single volume enclosed by a steel-framed, fireproof external wall. The steel structure absorbs all horizontal loads, while cardboard tubes take only vertical loads. This has allowed the junctions between the cardboard tubes and the floor to be designed very simply, as their only function is to prevent the columns from slipping. The tubes, which are made from recycled paper, form a peristyle along the length of the transparent south-facing wall. An opaque wall made up of continuous cardboard tubes screens the north wall and gently curves to meet the end of the peristyle. References are both Japanese and classical: paper is traditionally used in Japanese construction, and the curving wall is reminiscent of a bamboo forest. The columns provide a pattern of light and shade that changes throughout the day, invoking the shadows and columns of the agoras of ancient Greece.

Tubes along the southern wall are aligned with the upright sections of the steel frame.

**The curved wall of cardboard tubes is visible
through the south-facing glazed wall.**

Light fixtures and switches are accommodated
discreetly into the ceiling and walls.

Art Center College of Design
Library
1700 Lida Street
Pasadena, Calif. 91103

The ceiling casts a curved shadow on
the cardboard-tube wall, while the front
row of tubes casts stripes of shadow
across the floor.

Alberto Campo Baeza
CENTRO BIT
Mallorca, Spain

Building and landscape work as a single entity in this high-tech office by Albert Campo Baeza. Baeza has created a seamless environment by using the same finishes for internal and external spaces and by arranging structural elements and trees according to the same orthogonal 19.7-by-19.7-foot (6-by-6m) grid.

The triangular site is enclosed by a high stone wall finished internally in Roman travertine. The basement has been excavated, and the new floor slab established aboveground is also finished in travertine, so that the site reads as a triangular travertine box open to the sky. Enclosed space runs along the edge of the site, set apart from the perimeter wall. A "secret garden" of orange trees fills the remainder of the space. Frameless glazing has been used so that the enclosed space does not interrupt the continuous travertine ground plane, and cylindrical white metallic columns support the flat roof. Jasmine, wisteria, and grapevine which, like the orange trees, were chosen for their fragrance, have been trained to climb the walls. The conference room, which features tiered seating, has been excavated into the stone floor and covered by a glazed box. Service conduits flow through the basement, piercing through the ground to the workspaces.

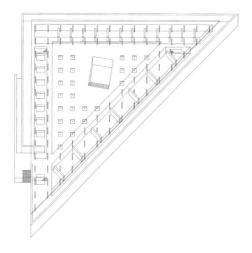

Steel columns are set apart from the glass walls and support the flat roof, which has a cantilever at each side.

A stone wall around the edge of the site shuts
out the surrounding industrial park.

Orange trees are set out according to the same grid as the columns.

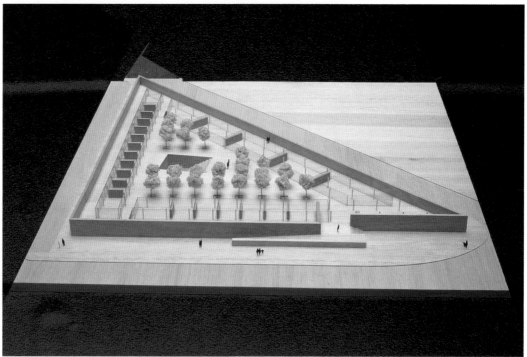

The model shot with the roof removed leaves structural elements clearly visible.

Frameless glazing to both sides creates
transparent internal space.

Branson Coates
OYSTER HOUSE
London, England

Designed as a prototype rather than a site-specific building, Oyster House has a structure that is organic, yet also simple and easily copied. The house is built on a grid of laminated softwood timber columns that have more than twice the strength of conventional solid timber; the insulated molded plywood tilted roof is clad in sheet copper. The building sits on a four-pointed, star-shaped timber deck, which is aligned to the corner windows and doors.

The ground floor is open, with choice of entry at any corner. The house is designed to suit a variety of family units, and the screens that divide the house in two can be fixed, movable, or absent, depending upon how many people live or work in the space and how closely they want to share the house. The upstairs is enclosed, but a continuous slit of window gives all-around views. Although the lower floor is fully glazed, it can be given varying degrees of privacy, either from veil-like curtains on a continuous curved track or with motorized roller-shutters, which are insulated for added protection from the cold and housed under the floor when not in use.

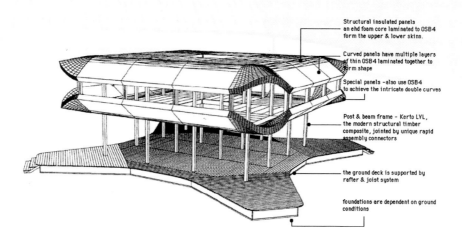

Structural insulated panels an ehd foam core laminated to OSB4 form the upper & lower skins.

Curved panels have multiple layers of thin OSB4 laminated together to form shape

Special panels –also use OSB4 to achieve the intricate double curves

Post & beam frame – Kerto LYL, the modern structural timber composite, jointed by unique rapid assembly connectors

the ground deck is supported by rafter & joist system

foundations are dependent on ground conditions

The building is supported by laminated softwood timber columns.

A computer-generated image of Oyster House shows upper-floor glazing sandwiched between copper-clad molded plywood, which acts as the roof and a canopy to the lower floor.

Two softwood timber staircases reinforce the symmetry and lead to opposite ends of the house.

Upstairs, an undulating floorscape provides an ideal environment for relaxation.

In this visually exciting computer-generated image,
veil-like curtains offer a degree of privacy to the
glazed lower floor.

Sauerbruch Hutton
PHOTONICS CENTRE
Berlin, Germany

At this center for scientific research, the structure is an integral part of the environmental strategy. Paired concrete columns around the perimeter of the main building are wide enough to support inner and outer glazed walls. This creates a cavity that acts as a thermal buffer zone in winter, and in summer becomes a solar chimney that helps to ventilate the offices. The narrow zone between the columns is used for air exhaust and the wide zone is used for air intake. Services rise in shafts along a central spine corridor, and are distributed horizontally within the prefabricated concrete U-shaped beams that form the floor/ceiling slabs. Removable units are set at right angles to the corridor. Their width is determined by the 23.6-foot (7.2 m) structural grid, but their lengths depend on the meandering of the facade.

This main three-story building has exposed concrete roof and floor slabs. An underground tunnel leads to the smaller single-story hall, which has a concrete roof slab supported by steel columns. Both buildings are protected from overheating and glare by colored blinds. As the blinds are electronically operated by occupants, the composition of the facade is in a constant state of flux.

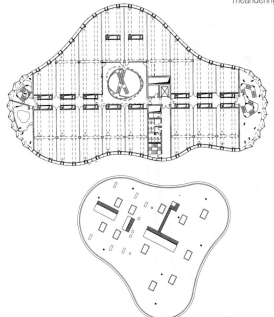

A central atrium is formed by openings in the thick concrete floors. The irregular, roughly circular shape of the openings is rotated at every floor to create a volume with shifting boundaries.

The towering entrance hall reveals the
full extent of the 52.5-foot (16 m) -high
painted concrete columns.

**The meandering facades visually reduce the
building's mass, and provide the main building
with units of varying length.**

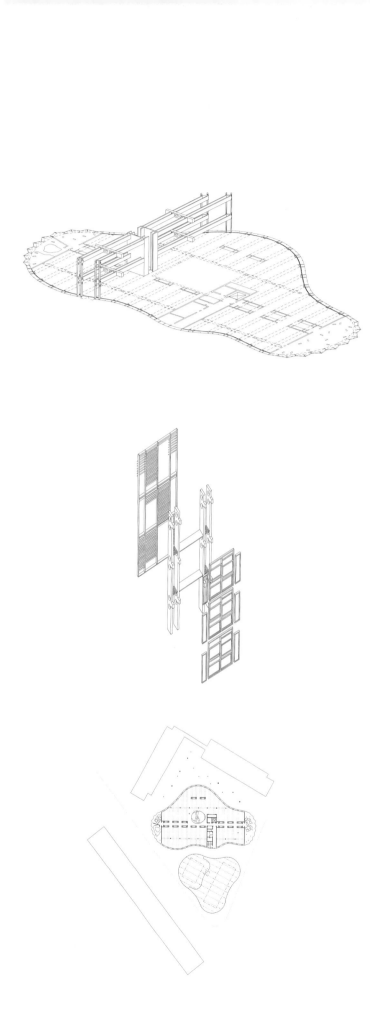

Color blinds provide protection from overheating and glare.

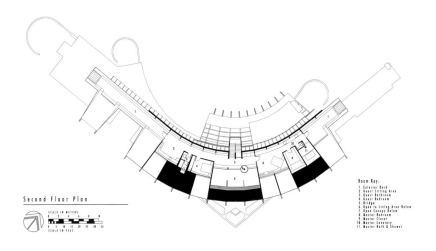

Second Floor Plan

SCALE IN METERS
0 2 4 6 10
SCALE IN FEET
0 5 10 15 20 25 30 35

Room Key:
1. Exterior Deck
2. Guest Sitting Area
3. Guest Bathroom
4. Guest Bedroom
5. Bridge
6. Open to Living Area Below
7. Open Canopy Below
8. Master Bedroom
9. Master Closet
10. Master Lavatory
11. Master Bath & Shower

Robert Harvey Oshatz

MIYASAKA RESIDENCE
Obihiro, Japan

In designing this home, Robert Harvey Oshatz used an expressive structure that frees the building from the constraints of rectilinear space. The lower floor is concrete, a favored material in Japanese construction, primarily due to its sense of permanence and strength. Where it supports the wooden structure above, the concrete is clad in stone. Elsewhere, it is left exposed, its surface chipped to soften its appearance.

Windows are expressed as voids between different structural components rather than as holes punched through walls. A continuous band of clerestory glazing gives the impression that the upper floor is floating above its base, and floods the interior with light even when the windows below are shaded for privacy. The upper floor consists of a radial cage of Alaskan yellow cedar glue-laminated beams bridged by square joists, and faced with plywood sheathing. The curve of the glulam beams provides earthquake resistance, and allows for a blurring of the distinction between ceiling, wall, and floor, resulting in a comforting, womblike space. This residence exploits the natural warmth of timber as both finish and structure.

The contrasting structures of the lower and upper floors are visible from the double-height living area.

Clerestory glazing brings light into
the ground floor.

Cabinetry of Douglas fir veneer is fitted with
countertops of granite or natural wood.

**Concrete is clad in stone where it supports
the wooden structure above.**

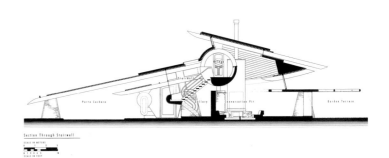

Section Through Stairwell

**Curved glulam beams create womblike
spaces and offer resistance to earthquakes.**

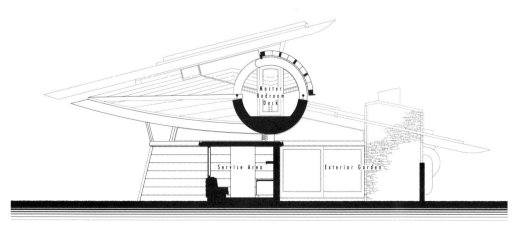

Master
Bedroom
Deck

Service Area   Exterior Garden

Section Through Service Area

SCALE IN METERS
0   1   2   3

0 1 2 3 4 5   10
SCALE IN FEET

Randy Brown
120BLO BUILDING
Omaha, Nebraska

Randy Brown has taken the steel frame typically used for spec offices, but subverted the way in which it is conventionally used. While the typical office building is a rectangular block built on a regular grid with a repetitive facade, the 120BLO Building is defined by a seemingly arbitrary placement of structural elements, with the exterior composed of abstract shapes and different finishes—outsize stainless steel shingles, glass, and planes of gray render.

A conventional office immediately reveals its size and form, but here structural elements are designed to conceal the nature of the area beyond, so that the space unfolds as the visitor moves through it. In place of the usual distinction between clear windows and solid walls, Brown uses materials of varying degrees of translucency or reflectivity. Steel shingles catch the light, while sloping walls of translucent polycarbonate allow light to filter through to the spaces beyond.

Steel beams and columns and a corrugated-steel roof are left exposed, with steel air-conditioning ducts adding to the industrial feel. The use of timber for the reception desk and floor gives the reception area a more homey feel.

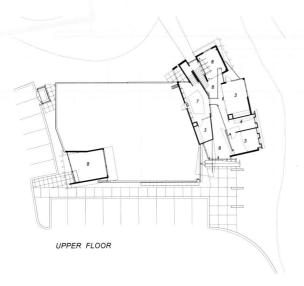

UPPER FLOOR

Shifting geometries and materials with varying degrees of translucency and reflectivity create spaces that are not instantly intelligible.

**Timber floors and reception desk
provide a note of familiarity among
the industrial materials.**

The doorway to the administrative area is framed by folded walls, giving the false impression of heavy masonry construction.

Daylight enters through skylights and is reflected off the stainless steel.

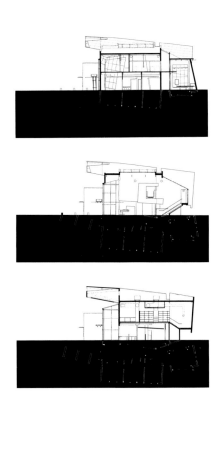

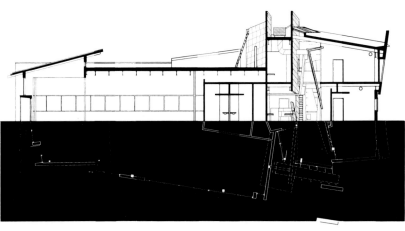

The different facade expressions contrast
with the repetitive facade typical of most
spec office buildings.

The conventional distinction between windows
and walls is blurred. The boundary of the
conference room is ambiguous.

William Bruder
PLATT RESIDENCE
Phoenix, Arizona

In designing this house for a metalworker, architect William Bruder played on the tension between the 3-inch (7.6 cm) -thick masses of desert stone and the full-span, spider-frame roof structure, which appears to be in a state of flight. The masonry walls are filled with cardboard lettuce-shipping containers, which are, in turn, filled with shredded computer printouts, achieving a mass similar to adobe. A ring of glass separates the walls from the spider-frame of the roof, which is made from oil-field drilling pipe weathered to an evenly rusted patina.

The building is based on a 30- to 60-degree grid that creates a series of triangular spaces, the largest of which is a living/eating area at the center of the house. At each of its three corners, there are smaller triangular spaces, two of which are sleeping areas and one the main entry. While the rusty-pipe roof structure follows this triangular grid, other materials are used in a way that counteracts it. The light ponderosa pine roof deck has a one-directional pattern, which is mirrored in the pattern of the $\frac{1}{8}$ inch brass joints in the polished concrete floors.

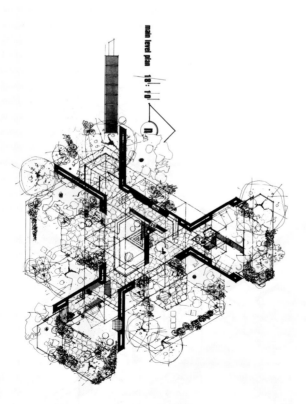

main level plan 1/8": 1'0"

Glass screens by the entrance door contrast with rough-hewn lumps of stone.

**Custom-made cabinetwork is of white oak,
with drawer fronts of stainless steel.**

Stone walls extend beyond the boundaries of the house, giving each sleeping area its own private courtyard.

**Stainless steel space-conditioning duct pylons
are expressed as sculptural volumes within
the interior.**

Future Systems
HOUSE
London, England

Future Systems conceived this family home in London as a glass slot between solid flank walls. Glass blocks give a robust feel to the street elevation, whereas the back wall, which faces the garden, is more fragile in appearance and is constructed of clear glass. This slanted double-glazed planar glass wall provides passive heating on winter days, and allows the family to feel in touch with the seasons. Internally, the structure is designed for maximum transparency. A durable white circular ceramic-tile floor emphasizes the link between internal and external spaces. Storage and bathrooms are in brightly colored core units, so that the only partitions required are glass fire screens between circulation and living space.

To achieve consistency, the same components are repeated throughout the house. Identical extruded-aluminum sections are used as beams over glass doors, as spines for the three aluminum staircases, to support the planar glazing, and as bracing for the glass-block wall. Although floors and ceilings have considerable mass to aid heat absorption, they have been designed to look lightweight. Where walls and ceilings meet, they are separated by aluminum or glass, and exposed ceiling edges are tapered to visually reduce their mass.

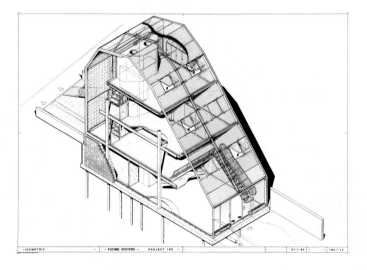

The three aluminum staircases are supported on an aluminum spine. White nylon plaited yacht cord is used for the balustrade.

White circular ceramic-tile floors give a light,
durable finish, and blur the distinction
between the ground floor and garden.

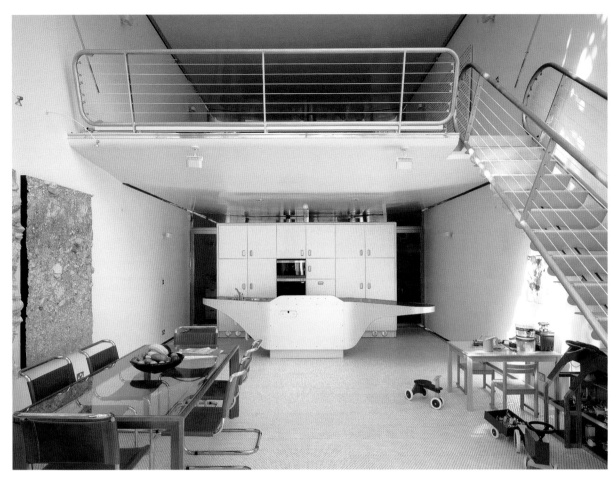

78

The edge of the mezzanine is tapered to
obscure its mass. Storage and bathrooms are
contained in brightly colored units, allowing
the rest of the house to remain as continuous
open-plan space.

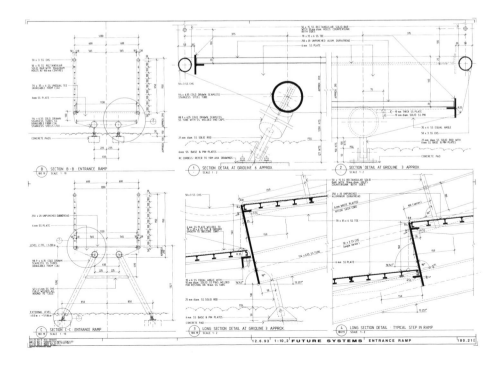

The slanting rear wall allows for a double-height living space, while minimizing the loss of daylight to the surrounding gardens.

PARK-KEEPER'S APARTMENT AND PARK LAVATORIES

Hyogo Prefecture, Japan

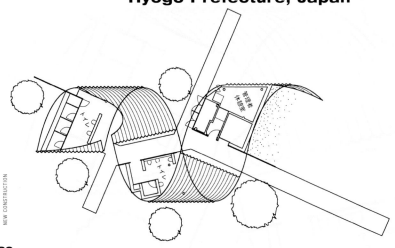

As this park-facilities building is surrounded by open space and positioned at the foot of a steep hill, it is designed to be viewed from every possible angle. Shuhei Endo responded to this challenge by bolting together curved sheets of corrugated metal to create a sculptural structure in which there is no clear distinction between back and front or roof and walls.

Natural materials are used so that the structure appears to have grown out of the landscape. Edges of the metal sheets pierce the earth through slots surrounded by piles of pebbles, and the glazed front wall of the flat rises out of a grass-covered earthwork. Inside the lavatories, pale brick walls and screens constructed from metal panels create a more industrial finish that is both low-maintenance and durable.

Set in a small park in the mountains of Hyogo Prefecture, this structure contains a park-keeper's apartment and two public bathrooms. The commission provided an opportunity to create an abstract focal point in a site that is surrounded by anonymous school buildings and had been devoid of architectural character.

Screens in the lavatories read as freestanding elements and do not detract from the drama of the metal coil.

Brick walls and metal screens give the
lavatories an industrial feel.

The grass-covered earthwork gives the park-keeper's apartment a degree of privacy by raising it above ground level.

The curved metal coil creates three
vaulted enclosures.

Mark Dziewulski
LAKESIDE STUDIO
Sacramento, California

Intended to be harmonious with the exterior landscape, this garden pavilion provides a tranquil and sheltered environment in which to enjoy the rich natural landscape, with its spectacular river views. Though the technical, structural detailing of the cantilevered building proved challenging, the final result presents an interior informed by the structure of the building.

The sculptural form of the structure curves and twists, taking advantage of the river views. A cantilevered floor stretches across the lake, providing occupants with a rich visual journey across the water. The experience of being on the water is heightened by areas of transparent glass flooring. The building is shaded by the dramatically extended roof overhang, which offers shelter to an otherwise visually open interior.

Uninterrupted glass walls open the room to the landscape. The extensive use of transparent glass dissolves the visual barriers between interior and exterior to give the space a sense of airiness. The design of the building also takes advantage of the play of natural light: sunlight reflecting off the water dapples the ceiling, constantly changing throughout the day; skylights punctuate the roof, bringing light deeper into the interior. The overall effect is contemplative and peaceful.

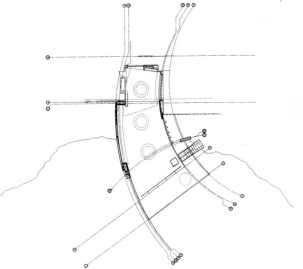

Inside the building, the experience is of floating out over the water.

Cantilevered beams and a concrete tower
act as bold, clean design elements as well as
supporting structures.

**A wall of angled translucent and transparent
glass panels creates an optical louver that
directs views away from the house.**

**Prism-like glass mullions separate large
sheets of glazing. Refracted light shafts
project an abstract light design across a
smooth marble floor.**

An overhanging roof and cantilevered floor,
supported by exposed beams, stretch out
over the river.

Skylights, strong sculptural shapes of their own, flood the studio with light.

RENOVATION

Frequently architects and designers are asked to renovate buildings, and the way they choose to incorporate the existing structure into the new design has a fundamental effect on the final result.

Tanner Leddy Maytum Stacy's Pennsylvania barn conversion and Tom Kovac's Melbourne Restaurant insert new, clearly defined objects within the shell of the existing building. Deborah Berke's New York offices and Meadowcroft Dernie's London house/gallery both work with existing structures, introducing pragmatic structural changes to meet the demands of the client, while London houses by Seth Stein and Chance de Silva and a London design studio by Allen-Gale all preserve remnants of the old as nostalgic momentos while creating buildings that are essentially new. Eduardo Souto de Moura's conversion of a Portuguese monastery into a hotel celebrates the existing structure while leaving ancient materials exposed. At the opposite extreme, Hanrahan+Meyers' New York apartment and Eichinger Oder Knechtl's apartment in Vienna are sleek modern spaces that treat the existing building simply as a shell that is all but invisible from the inside.

Eichinger oder Knechtl
MONOCOQUE, SCHRETTER APARTMENT
Vienna, Austria

By using movable screens to create a flexible space that contains all services, Eichinger oder Knechtl maximized space in this small apartment. At the entrance to this area, the bathroom is enclosed by stainless steel doors that allow access from both sides, but can also enclose the room within its own storage unit, leaving a route through to the main service space. One side is lined by a Ferrari net cupboard that houses the washing machine, while the other is lined by a folding net wall that can be folded to form a shower cubicle. The showers fittings are concealed within a metal column, while gaps in the American oak yacht floor are routed to form a water drain. An electrically-operated roof light allows the occupant to shower in the snow or rain. When the net wall is opened out, the shower disappears and the wall screens the wash basin, which sits in its own glass-box dormer window. The kitchen is a single unit that extends onto the balcony. The interior of the kitchen is made of oak, while the exterior is made of concrete, with space for a small, recessed herb garden.

The existing roof structure has been covered with metal and plasterboard, and part of the exterior wall has been replaced with a large, electrically-operated two-part window. The upper part tilts upward, while the lower part can slide outward to create a balcony space.

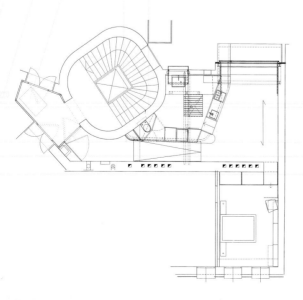

This view shows the kitchen area with the net wall folded to enclose the shower. The skylight allows the occupant to shower in the rain or snow.

When the folding net wall is opened out it screens
the sink and the shower disappears.

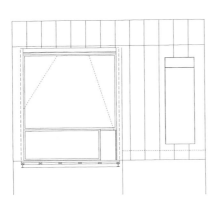
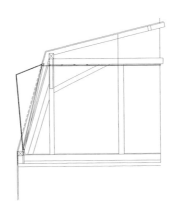

Housing all services in a single, flexible
living area creates clear, open spaces
in this small apartment.

The kitchen consists of a single unit, which extends outside the building. While the outdoor part of the unit is constructed of concrete, the indoor area is made of oak.

Steel doors define the passageway into the service area. Screened by net, the washing machine cupboard doubles as a translucent room divider.

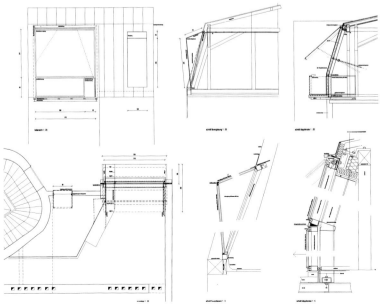

Hanrahan + Meyers
THE HOLLEY LOFT
New York, New York

The design for this lower-Manhattan second-floor loft conversion evolved out of several of Hanrahan + Meyers' previous projects, which used partial enclosures and transparent materials to explore the ambiguities between the exterior and interior. The Holley loft has no solid walls, so that the full dimensions of the apartment can be experienced from almost any position, and light from the windows at either end can penetrate deep into the space.

A single, full-height 48-foot (14.6 m) -long raw steel-and-glass wall marks the division between the master bedroom/bathroom and the rest of the apartment. Two sandblasted bays at the center of the wall provide the bathroom with privacy, and curtains can be pulled outward from this central area to screen the clear glass.

A 30-foot (9.1 m) -long maple cabinet opposite the steel-and-glass wall marks the boundary between the living spaces and the kitchen and guest bathroom, and a 40-foot (12.2 m) -long bookcase/storage cabinet runs along the rear wall. Full-height, movable, painted wood panels positioned close to this rear wall can be left as a freestanding objects, or can be used to create either one or two separate rooms, if required.

Full-height, painted wood doors can be used to create more intimate enclosed rooms.

The absence of solid walls leaves the entire
length of the apartment open to view.

Two sandblasted bays at the center of the main glass wall afford some privacy. This language of glass and steel is echoed in a portion of the maple cabinet that stands opposite.

A full-height steel-and-glass wall separates
the master bedroom and its bathroom from
the rest of the space.

Tanner Leddy Maytum Stacy
PRIVATE RESIDENCE
Chester County, Pennsylvania

The conversion of this 1820s barn draws a clear distinction between the old and new by accommodating new functions within a smooth cherrywood box that sits inside the existing 20-inch (50.8-cm)-thick fieldstone walls. Fireplaces, intimate seating areas, and white maple staircases are accommodated within the space between the rustic stone and the cherry plywood walls. A new steel structure supports the original hand-hewn oak beams that support the floors and roof. An opening in the floor of the middle story exposes the oak floor timbers and allows light to enter the rooms below, while the central portion of the upper floor is left as a void crossed by a steel, glass, and maple catwalk that hovers above the existing oak roof structure and connects the master bedroom to the dressing room. The roof has been perforated with skylights to minimize new openings in the walls. Existing ventilation slits at the second level are now windows, and arched apertures at the first-floor level have been fitted with steel windows and doors. A second-level threshing door has been replaced with a new door in the east wall, which leads onto a deck carved out of the roof of an existing porch.

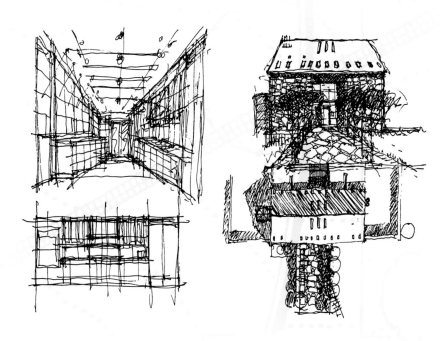

An opening in the second floor exposes the oak floor timbers and allows light to enter the rooms below.

Circulation space around the periphery of the
building is flanked by the original fieldstone
walls and the outer walls of the new cherry
wood box.

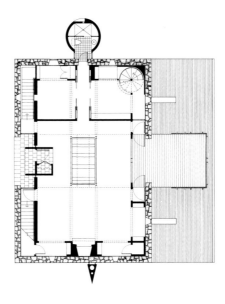

A new steel structure supports the original roof structure. The steel, glass, and maple catwalk hovers above the hand-hewn oak beams.

The smooth internal finishes of the new
insertion contrast with the rugged feel of
the existing oak and stone.

Meadowcroft Dernie
GALLERY AND PRIVATE RESIDENCE
London, England

In transforming an Edwardian pub into a gallery/home
for an art dealer, structural alterations were dictated by the
desire to bring natural light into the deep, narrow-fronted site.
Basement and ground-floor levels, which were previously
occupied by dark cramped rooms, have been turned into a
double-height dining room overlooked by a mezzanine library/study
and a gallery space with a double-height area where part of the
floor has been removed. To compensate for the shortage of windows,
Meadowcroft Dernie introduced a long roof light that illuminates the rear
wall of the double-height space and the long hall. Smaller skylights provide
patches of light in the study and dining room.

The floor above has been converted into a single space, which serves as the owner's
living room and features French doors that open onto a terrace on the gallery roof.
Finishes are simple-white walls and reclaimed oak floors provide a neutral backdrop for
works of art and complement the owner's bright, abstract furniture. Private rooms are on the
upper floors, and a new winding staircase leads to a wooden hut that opens onto the
uppermost roof terrace. The hut suggests an escape from the dense urban surroundings—its
construction is reminiscent of beach huts found on the English coast.

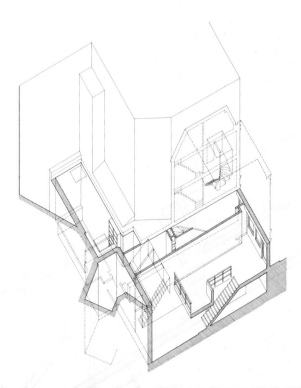

**The first floor living space contains the gallery
owner's personal collection and has the same
neutral finishes as the lower gallery floors.**

A concealed roof light illuminates the rear wall
of the double-height space.

Part of the existing floor has been cut away
so that both floors of gallery space can be
read as a single volume.

The roof light illuminates the otherwise
windowless hallway.

The mezzanine study overlooks a double-
height dining room, which fills space previously
occupied by two storerooms.

Seth Stein
COURTYARD HOUSE
London, England

Seth Stein built his own house on the site of an 1880s stableyard that was later used as a timber yard. A factory building that ran along the western edge of the site now houses the long kitchen/dining room, and a dilapidated stable block at the rear provides the brick walls of the upper-floor bedrooms as well as columns and beams in the living room underneath.

A perforated-metal gate opens onto a forecourt of white stones, with a timber deck leading to the house. Half solid and half glazed, this front wall is protected by a canopy of tapered louvers. Concrete floors and white plastered walls are punctuated with dashes of color, including a pink wall that marks the route from entrance to kitchen and an orange metal frame that encloses sliding doors. A frameless glass wall to the gallery and living room makes the stone, grass, eucalyptus, and miniature bamboo in the courtyard an integral part of the house itself. The linear geometry is disrupted by the sculptural curved stair and by a concrete cylinder that encloses a cloakroom and rises through the building to form a gazebo on the roof.

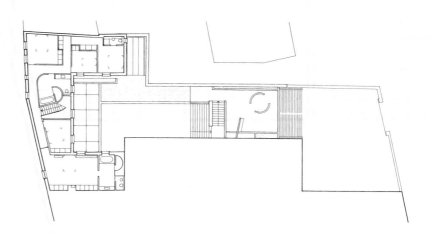

Views of the courtyard are encased by an orange metal frame that encloses the sliding door. A beam from the original stable block supports the glass roof and wall.

**The curved staircase reads as a sculptural
element, distinct from the main structure of
the house.**

The house is entered though a narrow pass
between the gray concrete cylinder and a
pink wall.

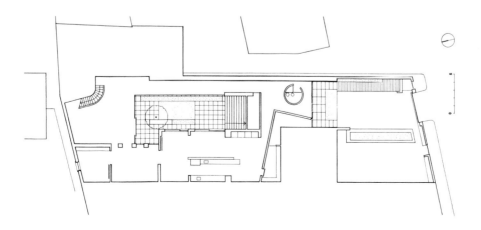

**Frameless glass forms the inner wall of the
long gallery and the living room, eliminating
visual barriers between inside and out.**

Eduardo Souto de Moura with Humberto Vieira
HOTEL CONVERSION FROM THE MONASTERY OF SANTA MARIA DO BOURO
Braga, Minho, Portugal

The Monastery of Santa Maria do Bouro consists of a church, parts of which date from the twelfth century, and a monastery set on a vast stone plinth, which was constructed between the sixteenth and eighteenth centuries. As part of Portugal's policy of revitalizing its ancient monuments, the monastery has been converted into a state-run hotel.

Hotel accommodation has been slotted into the existing walls of the monastery, and the plinth has been rebuilt as a terrace terminating in an austere stone pool. Eduardo Souto de Moura's work is concerned with expressing the essence of materials, and he has used stones from the site to rebuild the crumbling external walls while maintaining their earthy grain. Inside, stonework is either plastered or left exposed. Timber or stone floors and rusted-steel ceilings are unobtrusive, and services are imperceptible—heating, for example, is concealed beneath stone floors.

Elsewhere, new interventions contrast with the existing structure. En suite bathrooms are enclosed by timber screens, and the three bedroom levels are connected by a slender staircase of steel and wood. Metal balconies and glass doors set within crisp metal frames look particularly fragile when poised against the massive walls.

Timber floors make upstairs corridors more hospitable. Walls have been plastered, but windows and doorways reveal the original monumental stone.

Corten steel ceilings sit discreetly with the
stone structure.

A glass door with a thin metal frame contrasts
with massive stone walls. New stone stairs to
the terrace are expressed as a monolithic block.

From a distance, the monastery remains picturesque, giving no indication of its new use.

Stone and plain plastered walls give bed-rooms a monastic austerity. The bathroom is concealed behind the timber screen.

Bathrooms are sleek and modern but retain a simplicity that is in keeping with the building.

Chance de Silva
HOUSE CONVERSION
London, England

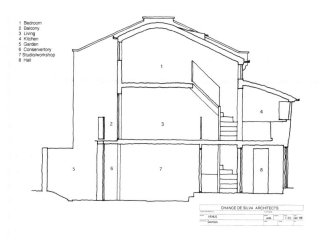

1 Bedroom
2 Balcony
3 Living
4 Kitchen
5 Garden
6 Conservertory
7 Studio/workshop
8 Hall

CHANCE DE SILVA ARCHITECTS

VENUS   wds   1:50   Jan 98

Section

Two young architects have built their own home on the site of a former garment manufacturer at the end of a row of nineteenth-century terraced houses. Bricks from the existing building were used for the party wall and for the bases of the front, rear, and side walls, while a timber frame has been used for the upper floors. The frame supports copper cladding, which wraps over the roof and around the gable wall so that the conventional distinction between roof and walls is replaced with a division between copper and brick. Seams on the copper cladding are angled at 45 degrees, contrasting with the vertical and horizontal lines of the brickwork.

The choice of materials combines a nostalgia for the building's former use with the architects' interest in Japanese design. Exposed brickwork and the galvanized steel balcony and stair are industrial in feel, and the kitchen is screened by a piece of vertically hung factory flooring.

Services are concealed in a shallow cupboard opposite the bathroom behind Japanese-style timber screens, and windows on the front and boundary walls are made from sheets of translucent paper encased in glass blocks, creating an effect similar to the paper screens used in Japanese homes.

An uplighter projects light off the gently curving ceiling.

Curved copper cladding wraps over the roof
and around the gable wall, creating a flamboyant
end to a nineteenth-century terrace.

While the rear elevation has clear glass
windows, the boundary-wall window consists
of a sheet of translucent paper encased in
glass blocks.

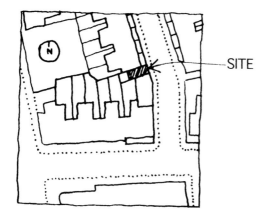

SITE

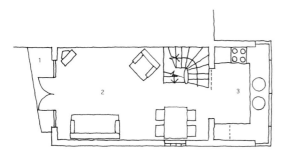

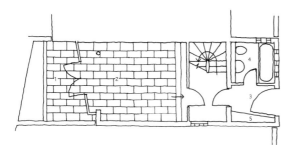

The steel staircase evokes the industrial
ethos of the building's past, while a piece of
vertically hung industrial flooring screens the
kitchen and provides pot-hanging space.

Allen-Gale Architects
BIG IDEA
MULTI-MEDIA
DESIGN CONSULTANCY
London, England

Faced with the challenge of converting a badly dilapidated building into space for a multimedia design consultancy, Allen-Gale decided to demolish everything except for the party walls and the elegant roof trusses. A new roof truss, indistinguishable from the others, has been added where an existing wall was removed. Sandblasted and repainted, these trusses now give the upper-floor studio its distinctive character.

Large steel doors recall the industrial nature of the original building, which was built in 1912 as a sawmill and coppersmith's workshop, and was more recently used as a hinge factory. A freestanding white wall separates a double-height entrance hall from the working spaces beyond, and conceals a concrete stair to the upper-floor studio. Continuous storage units conceal duct zones and run along both long walls of the open-plan studio space.

Bringing natural light into this long narrow building was a priority. The open-plan upper floor is flooded with natural light from full-length skylights, while on the ground floor a wall of acid-etched glass blocks allows natural light into an otherwise windowless meeting room. Both elevations are glazed, with clear glass at the upper-floor level and reinforced glass-block walling providing security at street level.

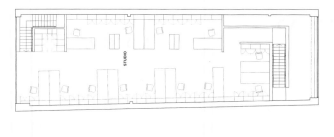

The 1912 roof trusses, now sandblasted and repainted, give the upper floor its character and are the only visible relics of the building's past.

A wall of acid-etched glass blocks is an
effective means of bringing natural light into
the otherwise windowless meeting room.

Glass-block walls are reinforced in both directions–the client's last offices were ram-raided three times.

**The staircase overlooks the double-height
entrance space.**

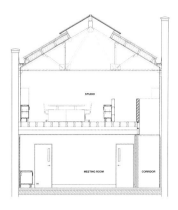

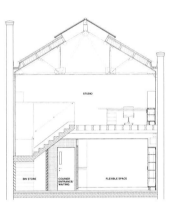

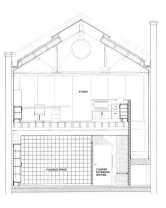

Tom Kovac
SAPORE
RESTAURANT
Melbourne, Australia

Tom Kovac
creates sensuous
organic buildings, that
read as seamless sculptural
spaces and conceal the secrets of
their construction. Sapore Restaurant has
been inserted into a two-story, double-fronted
Victorian building. Large glass doors set into the
simple white facade can swivel open so that the pavement
dining area becomes an extension of the inside. Internally, the
building has been stripped to a shell, and part of the upper floor has been
removed. A new interior has been created from sculpted plasterboard finished
in eggshell white. Existing stairs and passages have been retained but are hidden behind
the plasterboard. Services are also concealed, leaving a fluid white space, visually anchored
by an undulating black waxed plaster bar.

The soaring space contains two dining levels, with an existing beam forming a bridge which spans the
void above the bar and leads to a womblike hovering sixty-seat dining pod. Two deep elliptical openings in the ceiling let in
natural light, while flexible artificial lighting is provided by theater lighting brackets chosen for economy as well
as for dramatic effect.

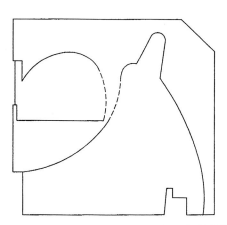

**A womblike dining room hovers precariously
over the main dining floor.**

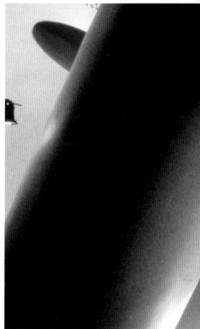

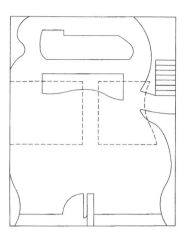

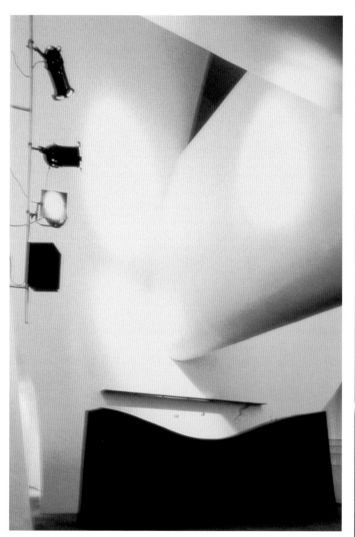

Flexible lighting is provided by theater-lighting brackets.

Dramatic patterns of shadow and light are
created by the theater lighting.

A black waxed plaster bar contrast with the
eggshell white, and visually anchors the
floating space.

Deborah Berke
BATTERY PARK CITY PARKS CORPORATION FACILITY
New York, New York

In designing new facilities for the Battery Park City Parks Corporation, Deborah Berke created distinct territories for the different activities that take place in the building, while making sure that all users feel connected to each other. Areas for different groups of staff or individual offices are enclosed by filing cabinets, work tables, and bookshelves, so that different teams are linked by walls of information rather than divided by solid walls. To fit the requisite 18,000 square feet of space into the existing 10,000-square-foot theater area, the building had to be divided into two floors. Glass blocks in the floor slab and double-height spaces in the work area and lounge create links between the two floors, and bring natural light into the basement-level lower floor.

As befits a non-profit, public-service organization, the design is no-nonsense and draws much of its impetus from existing structural elements. New materials were chosen for their durability, and services have been left exposed. Machinery and tools are very much on show, underscoring the public-service nature of the organization, while timber furniture provides a sense of warmth.

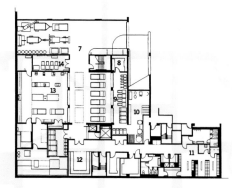

Double-height spaces connect the two levels and allow natural light into the lower ground floor.

Utilitarian materials are softened by the use of timber.

Internal windows create links between rooms and between floors.

The presence of machinery and tools underscores
the public-service nature of the organization.

Filing cabinets, work tables, and bookshelves
create boundaries between spaces. Upper and
lower floors are linked by a glass-block floor.

Directory

ALLEN-GALE ARCHITECTS

9 Northburgh Street
Clerkenwell
London EC1V 0AH
England

tel: 0044 171 566 9600

fax: 0044 171 253 5236

SHIGERU BAN ARCHITECTS

5-2-4 Matubara Ban Building, 1st Floor
Setagaya, Tokyo
Japan

tel: 0081 3 3324 6760

fax: 0081 3 3324 6789

ALBERTO CAMPO BAEZA ARQUITECTO

Almirante, 9
28004 Madrid
Spain

tel and fax: 00 349 1 521 7061

DEBORAH BERKE ARCHITECT

240 Lafayette Street # 1001
New York, NY 10012
USA

tel: 212 229 9211

fax: 212 989 3347

RANDY BROWN ARCHITECTS

6704 Dodge Street
Omaha, NE 68132
USA

tel: 402 551 7097

fax: 402 551 2033

WILLIAM BRUDER ARCHITECT

1314 West Circle Mountain Road
New River, AZ 85027
USA

tel: 623 465 7399

fax: 623 465 0109

CHANCE DE SILVA ARCHITECTS

1a Elfort Road
London N5 1AX
England

tel: 0044 171 690 4406

BRANSON COATES ARCHITECTURE

23 Old St
London EC1V 9HL
England

tel: 0044 207 336 1400

fax: 0044 171 490 0320

JAMES CUTLER ARCHITECTS

135 Parfitt Way SW
Bainbridge, WA 98110
USA

tel: 206 842 4710

fax: 206 842 4420

MARK DZIEWULSKI

2618 El Paseo Lane
Sacramento, CA 95821
USA

tel: 916 971 8900

fax: 916 971 8903

and
8 Victoria Rd
Walgrave
Berkshire RG10 8AB
England

tel: 0044 171 229 4535

EICHINGER ODER KNECHTL

Franzjosefskai 29
a1010 Wien
Austria

tel: 00431 5355424

fax: 00431 5354039

SHUHEI ENDO

SOAN 4F
1-7-13 Edobori
Nishi-ku, Osaka 550-0002
Japan

tel: 00 816 6445 6455

fax: 00 816 6445 6456

NEW CONSTRUCTION

156

STRUCTURE AS DESIGN

FUTURE SYSTEMS

21c Conduit Place
London W2 1HS
England

tel: 0044 171 723 4141

fax: 0044 171 723 1131

THOMAS HANRAHAN AND VICTORIA MEYERS ARCHITECTS

22 West 21 Street
New York, NY 10010
USA

tel: 212 989 6026

fax: 212 255 3776

TOM KOVAC
KOVAC/MALONE

1/422 Queen Street
Melbourne 3000
Victoria
Australia

tel: 0061 393 294 880

fax: 0061 393 294 881

DANIEL LIBESKIND

Windscheidstrasse 18
D-10627 Berlin
Germany

tel: 0049 30 324 9963 and 324 9835

fax: 0049 30 324 9591

MEADOWCROFT DERNIE ARCHITECTS

Unit A2, First Floor, Linton House
39-51 Highgate Road
London NW5 1RT
England

tel: 0044 171 692 2117

ROBERT HARVEY OSHATZ ARCHITECTS

12560 St. Elk Rock Road
Lake Oswego, OR 97034
USA

tel: 503 223 9258

fax: 503 635 4243

ANTOINE PREDOCK ARCHITECT

300 12 Street NW
Albuquerque, NM 87102
USA

tel: 505 843 7390

fax: 505 243 6254

SAUERBRUCH HUTTON ARCHITECTS

74 Ledbury Road
London W11 2AH
England

tel: 0044 171 221 01 05

fax: 0044 171 792 98 94

or
Lehrter Strasse 57
10557 Berlin
Gremany

tel: 0049 30 397 821 0

fax: 0049 30 97 821 30

SETH STEIN ARCHITECTS

52 Kelso Lane
London W8 5QQ
England

tel: 0044 171 376 0005

fax: 0044 171 376 1383

EDUARDO SOUTO DE MOURA

Rua do Aleixo No53
1 Esq, Porto 4150
Portugal

tel and fax: 00 351 2 618 7547

TANNER LEDDY MAYTUM STACY

444 Spear Street
San Francisco, CA 94105
USA

tel: 415 394 5400

fax: 415 394 8400

Photo Credits

Cover photo by Timothy Hursley

p. 1: photo by Bitter + Bredt Fotografie

p. 4: photo by Bitter + Bredt Fotografie

p. 5: photo by Richard Davies

p. 6-7: photo by Bitter + Bredt Fotografie

p. 8-9: photo by Trevor Mein Photography

p. 12-17: photos by Timothy Hursley

p. 18-23: photos by Bitter + Bredt Fotografie

p. 24-29: photos by Timothy Hursley

p. 30-35: photos by Hiroyuki Hirai

p. 36-41: photos by Hisao Suzuki and Raul del Valle

p. 42-47: photos © Branson Coates, by Philp Vile

p. 48-53: photos by Bitter + Bredt Fotografie

p. 54-59: Yoshiko Tobari, Warren McCutchen, Robert Harvey Oshatz

p. 60-67: photos by Randy Brown

p. 74-79: photos by Richard Davies

p. 80-85: photos by Yoshiharu Matsumura

p. 86-95: photos by Keith Cronin Photography

p. 98-103: photos © Margherita Spiluttini

p. 104-109: photos © Peter Aaron/Esto

p. 110-115: photos © Paul Warchol

p. 116-121: photos by David Grandorge

p. 122-127: photos by Richard Davies

p. 128-133: photos by Luis Ferreira Alves

p. 134-139: photos by Paul Tyagi

p. 140-145: photos by Graham Gaunt Photowork

p. 146-149: photos by Trevor Mein Photography

p. 150-155: photos © Paul Warchol

Index of Architects and Designers

About the Author

Isabel Allen trained as an architect before going into architectural journalism. Based in London, she is an award-winning journalist and editor of the *Architects' Journal*. Ms. Allen has been a visiting critic and lecturer at various schools of architecture in the U.K.

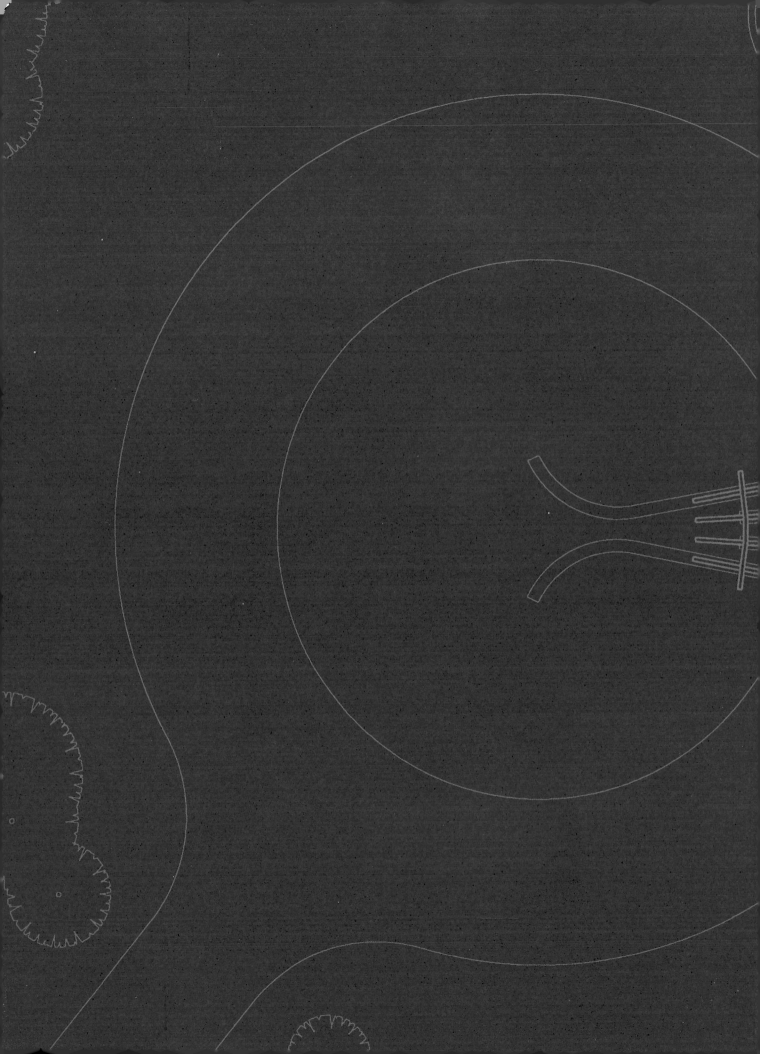